Ecosystems of North America

# The Mississippi River

## Maria Mudd Ruth

BENCHMARK BOOKS

MARSHALL CAVENDISH
NEW YORK

**With thanks to Dr. Dan Wharton, Central Park Wildlife Center, for his careful reading of the manuscript.**

Benchmark Books
Marshall Cavendish Corporation
99 White Plains Road
Tarrytown, New York 10591-9001

Illustration by Virge Kask
Map by Carol Matsuyama

Library of Congress Cataloging-in-Publication Data
Ruth, Maria Mudd.
     The Mississippi River / Maria Mudd Ruth.
        p. cm. — (Ecosystems of North America)
     Includes bibliographical references (p. ).
     Summary: Describes the course of the largest river in North America, the Mississippi and the connections between the plant and animal species that live in and around it.
        ISBN 0-7614-0934-3
        1. Stream ecology—Mississippi River—Juvenile literature. 2. Mississippi River—Juvenile literature.
    [1. Mississippi River. 2. Stream ecology. 3. Ecology.] I. Title. II. Series.
        QH104.5.M5M84     2001     577.6'4'0977—dc21     99-049873

**Photo Credits**
Photo research by Candlepants Inc.
Cover photo: DDB Stock Photo © C. C. Lockwood
The photographs in this book are used by permission and through the courtesy of:
© Clint Farlinger: 4–5, 9, 38. Photo Researchers, Inc.: © Tom & Pat Leeson, 10; © Jim Wark, 11; © Gregory K. Scott, 16 (left), 24–25, 52; © William H. Mullins, 16 (right); 19; © Rich Treptow, 21; © Harry Engels, 26; 29; © Suzanne L. Collins & Joseph T. Collins, 30, 47; © Fletcher & Bayles, 31; © Len Rue Jr., 32; © David R. Frazier, 40, 67; © John Mitchell, 48; NASA/Science Source, 51; © Tom McHugh, 54. Corbis-Bettmann: © Richard Hamilton Smith, 14; © Kevin Fleming, 34–35; © David Muench, 46. © Richard Hamilton Smith: 18, 28, 64–65, 66, back cover. DDB Stock Photo: © C. C. Lockwood, 27, 33, 42, 44–45, 58, 60; © D. Donne Bryant, 56–57, 62, 63. Lyndon Torstenson: 37. The Nature Conservancy: 43. Animals Animals: © Park A.-Surviva OSF, 49.

Printed in Hong Kong
6   5   4   3   2   1

# Contents

# The Mighty Mississippi

It is the largest river in North America. It flows from northwestern Minnesota to the Gulf of Mexico—a distance of 2,348 miles (3,779 km). It nearly splits the United States in two, with Minnesota, Iowa, Missouri, Arkansas, and Louisiana on its west bank and Wisconsin, Illinois, Kentucky, Tennessee, and Mississippi on its east. From these ten states and twenty-one others stretching from the Rocky Mountains to the Appalachians, this mighty river collects massive amounts of rainwater and snowmelt.

To explore the Mississippi, let's begin where it begins—at its **source** or **headwaters**, a lake in northwestern Minnesota. Here, on one side of the lake, a river has broken through the bank. It is a mere trickle of a stream. Shallow and only 10 feet (3 m) wide, who would guess it's the Mississippi? As it leaves the lake, it flows over a series of stepping stones marking the beginning of its journey. You could walk across it in less than a minute. But why rush? Imagine yourself taking off your shoes and walking onto the stepping stones. When you are halfway across, get your balance, and face the river. Your heels are in Lake Itasca, and your toes are in the Mississippi River. The water is cool and clear. From this point, 1,475 feet (442.5 m) above

*Flowing gently from its source at Minnesota's Lake Itasca, the Mississippi River begins its long journey and powerful influence on all living things within its reach.*

sea level, the river flows swiftly downhill. On its journey, it flows in and out of a series of lakes. It swallows new rivers and streams that enter it from the east and west. As it rolls through Minnesota and Wisconsin, it doubles, triples, and then quadruples in size. It tumbles through forests, over falls and rapids, and plunges into rock gorges. It cuts its way deep into the land, creating steep bluffs on each side. It carves its course past farms, towns, and cities in Iowa, Illinois, and Missouri. It becomes a wide and muddy river. It creates islands and sand bars, rushing around them, then washing them away. It winds through prairies and parklands. As it cuts across the flatlands of Kentucky, Tennessee, Arkansas, and Mississippi, it flows back and forth across the land in great curves called meanders. Then as it nears sea level, it loses much of its power. It settles across Louisiana, releasing its water into small creeks and channels. At Louisiana's southeastern tip, the Mississippi flows out onto a narrow arm of land where it splits into five small channels that splay out like the fingers on a hand. Through these channels, the river moves slowly, almost reluctantly, toward the ocean where the outgoing tides draw it into the salty waters of the Gulf of Mexico.

In 1832, explorer Henry Schoolcraft, guided by an Ojibwe chief, discovered the true headwaters of the Mississippi River—Lake Itasca in Minnesota. The name "Itasca" was created from two Latin words: verITAS meaning "truth" and CAput meaning "head."

This is one simple story of the Mississippi River. Actually, it is only one version of the water's path in one part of the river. That part is the main **channel**, the heart of the system where the river runs deepest and carries the most water. This is the blue squiggly line that you see on the map. But the Mississippi is more than its main channel, and it is much more than water. As it flows from Minnesota to Louisiana, it is constantly changing its shape, size, and course. From the northern hardwoods to the southern bayous, it is an accommodating host to the vast array of creatures that live in and around it.

## Choosing a Neighborhood

The Mississippi River is teeming with life. Hundreds of different species, or kinds, of animals and plants live in the river's channel.

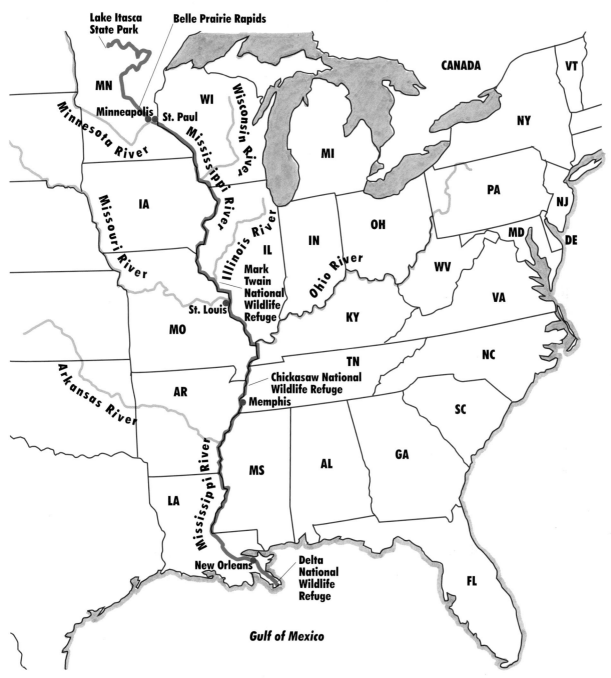

# The Mississippi River

The Mississippi is at the heart of a vast network of waterways. The Minnesota, Wisconsin, Illinois, Missouri, Ohio, and Arkansas Rivers are some of the major tributaries that funnel water to the river and link it, in turn, to communities far beyond the Mississippi's banks.

These plants and animals are **aquatic** organisms. But they don't live just anywhere along the entire length of the Mississippi. In choosing their surroundings, they fulfill certain needs such as the temperature and depth of the water. They might require certain kinds and amounts of nutrients in the water. A rocky river bottom may be ideal as opposed to a sandy one. They may have to be with certain other kinds of organisms. All of these needs help determine where they live along the Mississippi, or their **habitat**. A habitat is the place that has all the living and nonliving things that an organism needs to grow. The Mississippi offers a variety of aquatic habitats in its main channel, from shallow and swiftly flowing rapids to deep, slow-moving waters.

But the main channel of the Mississippi doesn't always stay within its banks. It floods, or overflows, its sides. It wanders onto the **floodplain**, the usually flat land that lies beside the river. Here, it carves lakes and side channels, builds up and washes away islands, makes detours and shortcuts for itself, and creates wetlands such as marshes and swamps. Hundreds of different species of animals and plants live in the river's floodplain, in **flood zone habitats**. These habitats may be alternately wet, dry, or soggy for all or parts of the year. The animals that live here may be aquatic, semiaquatic, or terrestrial (land dwelling). Fish are aquatic animals that live in the water held in the floodplain. Beavers are semiaquatic animals; they live in the river and on the land next to it. Fox and deer are terrestrial animals, but they use the river for their drinking water. Many insects live part of their lives in the river and part of it in the air and on the land around it. Clearly, animals use the river in a variety of different ways.

Within the aquatic habitats and the flood zone habitats, plants and animals live together, forming **biological communities**. Each community of living and nonliving things interacts to create an ecological system, or **ecosystem**. A person who studies the relationships among different species of plants and animals in their environment is called an **ecologist**.

## Flowing with Food

The water in the Mississippi cannot sustain life by itself. Living things must trap energy from the sun. They use this energy for growth,

*White-tailed deer rely on the Mississippi for their drinking water. Hundreds of tributaries, snowmelt, and rainfall contribute millions of gallons to this massive liquid pipeline.*

warmth, or movement. Then they release it. On land, green plants do most of the trapping. Through a process called **photosynthesis**, they use sunlight, carbon dioxide, and water to make sugars and other substances. In certain parts of the river where the current is slow and the sunlight can penetrate the water, tiny floating plants called **phytoplankton** grow. But the river is generally too swift to support enough phytoplankton to supply all the necessary energy. So how do other forms of energy get into the water? Green, energy-rich plants and leaves fall, blow, or flow into the river from the land. Once they arrive, bacteria and fungi attack them, turning the once-living plants into decaying matter called **detritus** (de TRY tiss). Detritus includes all the remains of plants as well as animals (who ate the plants) in the river.

In aquatic ecosystems, most of the energy comes from detritus. Small insects, crustaceans, clams, and other organisms consume the detritus and the nutritious bacteria and fungi. These organisms are called **detrivores**. They use a share of the plant's energy to grow. A fish will eat one of these detrivores and use the energy to swim against the river current. The fish is a **predator** because it consumes other animals. The fish loses some of the energy in the form of waste it releases into the water. This, too, is detritus. A great blue heron or a bald eagle, also predators, might catch that fish and use its energy for flying. The parts of the fish they don't eat become detritus, too.

The energy from the sun flows through a **food chain**. This pathway describes feeding relationships in which one species is eaten by another species that is, in turn, eaten by another. These feeding relationships help shape and define the river's biological communities.

Detritus, the first link in many food chains, is moved downstream by the river's current, like a giant conveyor belt at the grocery store. The leaves and plants that fall into the river are carried miles away. Animals that eat the leaves eventually die and decompose and are moved along the conveyor belt to another part of the river even farther downstream.

*Where fish are plentiful, bald eagles hunt in the river and take their place at the top of the aquatic food chain.*

The Mississippi River is also constantly moving many other things. It transports **sediment**, that is, solid matter ranging in size from boulders to fine particles of sand, silt, and clay. Sediment comes from many different sources. Some of it is produced by the river itself as it erodes its banks and channel. Sediment also enters the river in huge quantities as soil that erodes or washes into the water from farmland, overgrazed cattle pastures, construction sites, and other areas where the land has been stripped of the trees and plant cover that hold the soil together. Some of it is carried by rainwater and snowmelt that runs off the land instead of soaking into the soil. This **runoff** may flow directly into the Mississippi or enter the river from its **tributaries**. A tributary is a stream that feeds, or flows into, a larger stream. The Mississippi's tributaries range in size from tiny trickles of water to major rivers such as the Missouri, Ohio, and Illinois.

*Trees and plants prevent the erosion of soil into the water. But at industrial sites where they have been stripped away, sediment chokes the river and the lives it supports.*

The river also carries hundreds of different chemicals. Many are a natural part of the river; others are not. Through surface runoff, tributaries, and pipelines, pollutants from industries, homes, farms, and roadways enter the river in great quantities. These pollutants include pesticides, fertilizers, gasoline, motor oil, toxic chemicals, sewage, bacteria, and viruses. Many of these make the river unsafe or hazardous for humans, wildlife, and plants. The amounts and kinds of chemicals, sediments, and nutrients in the Mississippi change constantly. Often only the big changes, such as oil spills, are reported in the news. But smaller changes and those that occur slowly over many years have had a greater impact on the living communities of the Mississippi.

## Human Life on the Mississippi

People are part of the Mississippi River ecosystem, too. Early Native American cultures came to the river to hunt and fish. In about 1000 B.C. they began to settle and farm the rich soils of the Mississippi floodplain. Trade routes were established up and down the river. Many cultures flourished along the river. Around A.D. 1000, people known as the Mound Builders established settlements throughout the floodplain. They piled earth in round heaps, in the shapes of animals or in great squares. Some of their settlements can still be seen today along the river in large and complex cities built on earthen mounds. Many tribal cultures, such as the Dakota, Sioux, and Chippewa, lived along the river in villages, using the river to supply food and as a long-distance transportation route.

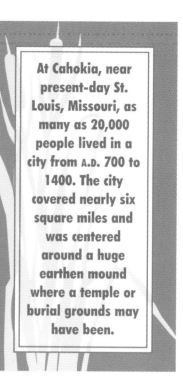

At Cahokia, near present-day St. Louis, Missouri, as many as 20,000 people lived in a city from A.D. 700 to 1400. The city covered nearly six square miles and was centered around a huge earthen mound where a temple or burial grounds may have been.

In the 1600s, the river was first explored by Europeans who introduced great changes to the native cultures and to the entire river ecosystem. Wildlife was trapped and hunted, and many of the forests were cleared with little thought given to the consequences. By the 1800s, towns, cities, and industries lined the riverbanks and used the Mississippi to carry away their wastes. Dams were built across the river to deepen its channel for shipping. High earthen walls were built alongside the river to stop it from flooding. Its floodplains became places for crops and buildings. Today, few places on the Mississippi River could be considered "natural." The impact of human activities can be seen on every stretch of the river. The Mississippi River ecosystem of five hundred years ago is a much different one today. Still, it is an ecosystem worth preserving and exploring. Our examination begins with the rapids, heading through shallow pools, river-fed ponds, and soggy delta marshes, where the Mississippi meets the sea.

# Two Views of the Mississippi

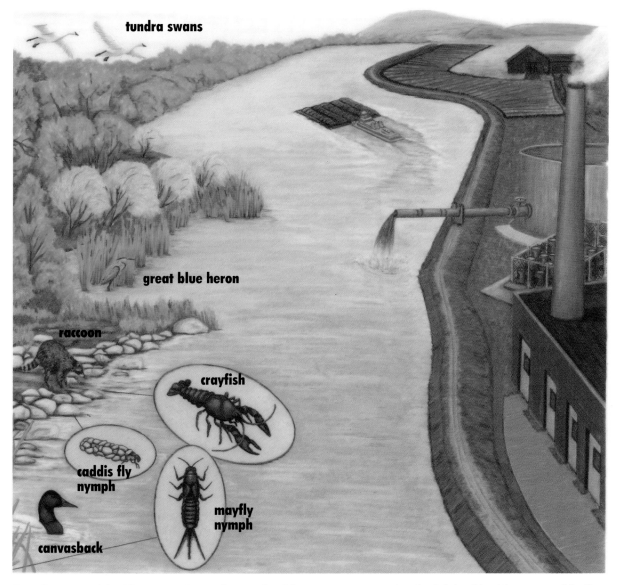

tundra swans

great blue heron

raccoon

crayfish

caddis fly
nymph

mayfly
nymph

canvasback

*This drawing of the Mississippi River shows a healthy river ecosystem (on the left bank) with a natural buffer of aquatic plants and trees that offer food and habitat for a variety of wildlife. On the right bank, the river has been dredged for shipping channels, leveed to prevent flooding, and used as dumping sites for factory waste. A river altered in this way loses its ability to support an ecosystem or sustain life.*

# Life in the Rapids

You are standing on the banks of the Mississippi in central Minnesota at a place called Belle Prairie Rapids. The water is clear and shallow—just 2 to 3 feet deep (.6–.9 m). In this stretch of the river, the water flows rapidly and splashes over the rocky bottom. Large stands of centuries-old pine trees as well as oaks, ash, and maple trees grow on the shoreline and on upstream islands. Aquatic grasses thrive along the banks. Scattered across the bottom of the river are small boulders and scores of round, highly polished rocks about the size of your fist. From the edge of the river, you reach into the water and pick up a small rock near the bank and turn it over. What you see on the bottom of the rock is surprising: lots of little things with legs and tails, squirming around, trying to get back to the underside of the rock. These "things" are insects. They have a big name and a big job to do in the Mississippi River ecosystem.

## Spineless Wonders

First, the big name. These insects belong to a group of animals called **benthic macroinvertebrates**. "Benthic" simply means that they live on the bottom

*Fast-flowing and full of life, sections of the Mississippi race by as rapids tumbling over everything in their path.*

(benthos) of the river. "Macro" means they are big enough to see with the naked eye (without a microscope). And "invertebrate" means they do not have a backbone (vertebrae). What you saw under the rock were mayflies, stone flies, and caddis flies—three of the hundreds of kinds of benthic macroinvertebrates found in the Mississippi River. The life cycle of these insects includes stages as an egg, larva, pupa, and adult. They spend the first three stages in the river. When you see them squirming around on rocks, they are in their larval stage— soft-bodied, wingless, aquatic insects. Like fish, they breathe the oxygen that is dissolved in the water. Some species breathe through gills that may appear as feathery, brushlike, or platelike attachments on their bodies. Others breathe directly through their thin body wall. These larvae live and grow underwater, then hatch into flying airborne adults.

Few insects live in rapidly flowing water, but our trio of larvae have developed **adaptations**, or special features that help them survive in this turbulent environment. They have flattened or streamlined body shapes so water flows over them more easily. They spend most

Pollution-sensitive mayflies are a sign of a clean river and a healthy food chain. Predators threaten this newly hatched adult from all sides. It must avoid becoming a meal for a fish, frog, or bird.

Stone flies spend most of their lives on the river bottom, where they shred and consume decaying leaves and other detritus.

of their time on the bottom and sides of rocks where the current is slower. Here, they cling to the rocks with their six legs and hairlike tails sprawled (much the way human rock climbers spread out their arms and legs to cling to the side of a cliff). Hooks on the ends of their legs increase their clinging ability. Many caddis flies build cases around themselves out of bits of rock, leaves, or small sticks bound together with the silk they produce. They attach these cases firmly to a rock and live inside them. Each rock at Belle Prairie can serve as home to several different macroinvertebrates—sprawlers, clingers, and case makers alike. Some people think that a river full of "bugs" is dirty or polluted. But these bugs are part of a clean river and a healthy ecosystem.

Now for the big job they perform. Like insects and crustaceans, these macroinvertebrates are detrivores. But they don't simply eat the detritus. The macroinvertebrates have specialized mouthparts to shred, scrape, filter, and gather the detritus. Upstream, where the detritus enters the current, shredders are abundant. As they eat, they tear the detritus into smaller and smaller pieces—much the way a garbage disposal grinds up food so it can flow down the kitchen drain. The current, the Mississippi's built-in conveyor belt, carries this nutritious shredded matter downstream to places such as Belle Prairie where there is little tree cover to deposit leaves directly in the stream. Many of the macroinvertebrates here specialize in collecting and filtering shredded detritus with the fine hairs on their legs or mouths or in the webs they build in the spaces between rocks. In the sunnier places in the stream, where the light may encourage the growth of algae, scrapers who graze in the algae and remove it from the rocks dominate the macroinvertebrate community.

All of these different eating styles means that there is no competition for food. Many macroinvertebrates can coexist on one rock, with some scraping algae, some filtering food from the flowing water, and others shredding leaves stuck to the rock. Algae scrapers do not compete with filter feeders because each species has body and mouthparts designed either to scrape or to filter, but not both. And by minimizing competition, these different eating styles maximize the insects' survival in other ways. The algae scrapers reduce the amount

*Energy from the sun is trapped in leaves, which blow or fall into the river. Like a giant conveyor belt, the Mississippi carries tons of this nourishing matter to communities downstream.*

of algae in the river; uncontrolled algae could reduce the level of dissolved oxygen in the water to a point where many macroinvertebrates would die. The shredders help by processing the food necessary for the survival of the filter feeders living downstream.

No matter how they feed, the macroinvertebrates are food for many other larger aquatic creatures. Smallmouth bass, walleye, carp, suckers, and catfish feed on the macroinvertebrates either as larvae or as adults flying above the stream and landing on the water. These fish attract birds such as herons, which wade at the river's edge and kingfishers and bald eagles, which swoop down to the river to hunt. The macroinvertebrates are just tiny members of a far-reaching chain.

*A belted kingfisher perches above the river, ever on the lookout for fish. A well-timed plunge headfirst into the water may mean a meal for this small, common bird.*

## How Clean Is the Water?

Macroinvertebrates also play an important role in indicating whether the river is clean or not. Stone flies, mayflies, and caddis flies require very clean water. If the water is polluted with chemicals, overloaded with sediment, too warm, or has low levels of dissolved oxygen, the macroinvertebrates simply die. They cannot swim away or otherwise escape polluted water (the way a fish or bird can), so their presence indicates clean water. Their presence is also the sign of a healthy ecosystem. They feed on detritus, so we know there must be trees and other plants nearby. They have delicate gills, so the water must be free of heavy sediments, which would clog these gills and suffocate the insects. They live attached to rocks, so we know a blanket of sediment must not be covering the rock surfaces. They are also part of a food chain that includes birds, fish, and other aquatic animals, so the presence of one member of the chain is a good indication that all the links are thriving. Elsewhere on the Mississippi, where the macroinvertebrates are less abundant or are nowhere to be found, we can assume the river is polluted and that the ecosystem is facing some serious threat.

One the most serious problems in the Mississippi today is the increase in sediments entering the river. As more and more land is cleared for development and agriculture along the Mississippi and its tributaries, soil washes easily into the river. This sediment also carries nutrients. In certain amounts, nutrients are essential to ecosystems. In excess, they act as pollutants. Nutrients enter the Mississippi as fertilizers used on agricultural lands, golf course grass, and suburban lawns and gardens. They arrive in the form of human and animal waste transported by runoff or from sewage treatment plants. They seep in as detergents containing phosphates. And they occur in ever-increasing amounts as towns, cities, and their populations grow. Too many nutrients cause the rapid growth of algae, which "blooms" in big mats that float on top of the water and cover the rocks below.

> By 1860, 735 steamboats operated daily on the Mississippi River near St. Louis and their fuel consumption (oak, beech, ash, or chestnut) was enormous. One historian estimated the daily fuel needs of a single large steamboat was equal to the amount needed to construct fifteen small frame houses.

When the algae dies, it uses up huge quantities of oxygen. And a river with low oxygen levels spells sudden death for macroinvertebrates. The loss of this food source results in a decline in the populations and diversity of the small aquatic creatures, fish, and birds that are part of this aquatic food web. The river becomes empty except for a thick carpet of algae and pollution-tolerant insects such as mosquitoes and blackflies. The disruption of even the slightest part of a food chain sends shock waves through the entire community.

With pollutants coming in so many disguises, it is hard to bar all their paths into the river. Pollutants also come in the form of pesticides, herbicides, motor oil, household chemicals, gasoline, lead, mercury, and hundreds of others toxic chemicals. They enter the water from a variety of sources, such as an industrial waste pipe, a sewage pipe, from runoff, and from the Mississippi's many tributaries. The

*Green algae is a natural part of a river system, but in excess quantities it can deplete the water's oxygen supply and threaten the lives of countless organisms.*

Mississippi and most of the rivers in the country were once so polluted with chemicals, sediment, and nutrients that the United States Congress passed the Clean Water Act of 1972 to begin controlling water pollution. Since then, the overall water quality of the Mississippi has been slowly improving, but it will take many more years to determine if the entire river can be restored to the fishable, swimmable conditions the act proposes.

## Watching the River

How could we find out if our clean river at Belle Prairie was becoming polluted? A team of science students from Little Falls Community High School near Belle Prairie has been watching the river since 1991. They are part of a nationwide network of students, teachers, and community volunteers who are checking up on the health of the Mississippi, its tributaries, and other rivers throughout the United States.

Twice a year, the Little Falls students visit Belle Prairie to measure levels of dissolved oxygen and the amount of sediment and other contaminants. But they rely on the macroinvertebrates to get the real picture of the ecosystem's health. They collect, identify, and count the macroinvertebrates from several places in the rapids. If the team finds hundreds of mayflies, stone flies, and caddis flies (which they usually do), they give the river a clean bill of health. If they notice a sudden or unusual drop in the numbers of macroinvertebrates, they suspect an imbalance in the ecosystem. Before the problem can work its way up the food chain, they report their findings immediately and work to fix the problem.

The bad news and the good news they report is used by several local and state government organizations responsible for the area's water and land use: pollution controllers, water planners, natural resource managers, and soil conservationists. There is a growing number of concerned citizens from the United States, Canada, and Mexico joining river-monitoring groups to keep a close eye on their local streams and rivers. With the information provided by these groups, wise decisions and long-term plans can be made about how to use and protect the Mississippi, its tributaries, and the land they flow through.

# Clear Water or Clean Water?

Water that is clear is not always clean. Water with dirt in it is not always polluted. Water we think is clean may not be able to support life. In this experiment you and your classmates and friends can use your senses of smell and sight to tell the difference between clean and clear water. You will need:

- 4 clear glass or plastic jars
- labels
- tap water
- bottled spring water
- pond or stream water
- 1 tsp. clear oil such as baby oil or mineral oil
- a few drops of rubbing alcohol or nail polish remover
- paper and pens or pencils

1. Fill one jar with cold bottled spring water and label it #1. Fill one jar with tap water and label it #2. Fill one jar with tap water and add one teaspoon of clear oil to jar #3. Fill one jar with tap water and add a few drops of rubbing alcohol or nail polish remover and label it #4. Fill one jar with water from a nearby pond or stream and label it #5. (If there is no stream or pond nearby, you can fill a jar with tap water, a scoop of dirt and some small rocks or pebbles. Let this sit for a few hours so the dirt can settle.)

2. Place the jars on a table and have each participant write numbers one through five on their paper. Take turns writing down how the water smells and looks and if you think the water can support living organisms.

3. Share your answers and discuss why you chose them. The person setting up the jars (you or a supervising adult) can reveal the answers below once everyone has discussed their own responses.

4. Jar #1 (spring water) is clear and clean and could support life.

   Jar #2 (tap water) is clear, but not clean as it contains chemicals such as chlorine used to kill bacteria. The amount of chlorine is too small to harm those who drink it, but it will kill bacteria, and aquatic organisms such as phytoplankton, macroinvertebrates, and fish.

   Jar #3 (oil) is clear but has a distinct odor that indicates it is polluted with chemicals. The oil also makes the water look polluted as the oil floats on the top of the water.

   Jar #4 (alcohol or nail polish remover) is also clear, but has an odor that indicates it is polluted. This water could not support life and is toxic to humans and animals as drinking water.

   Jar #5 is not clear and it may have an odor (like dirt or rotting leaves), but it is not polluted and can support life. Water from a stream or pond is never clear and is often full of tiny organisms such as bacteria, algae, and fungi and detritus that are the foundation for an aquatic food chain. If your water is from a pond or stream, look at it closely and you may see tiny organisms or even macroinvertebrates in the water. If your jar #5 contains spring water, dirt, and rocks, leave the jar open in a sunny window (during colder weather) or outside (during warmer weather). Over the next few weeks, examine the water in the jar. You may find algae growing on the sides of the jar and small creatures squirming around in the water.

# Slowing the Flow

*A*s you stroll along the shoreline at Minnesota's Lake Itasca State Park, the sound of the babbling Mississippi River follows you. Next to this tranquil ten-foot-wide (3 m) river, pine trees, aspen, black willow, pin cherry, and ash abundantly grow. You can imagine what it might have been like when Native American cultures— the Dakota and Chippewa—camped here thousands of years ago to hunt, fish, and trap in the forest and the water. They would move on foot and in canoes made of birch bark or dugouts carved from the trunk of a tree. The forests were filled with timber wolf, bison, black bear, and coyote in the forests. There were mink, otter, and beaver swimming the rivers, ponds, and lakes.

As you continue walking, the sound of the river changes. It is quieter. The forest has changed, too. It is lighter. You stop and look around. The trees are gone, and there seems to be a pond in the middle of the river. You approach the pond slowly. A loud slapping sound on the water startles you. You turn and catch a glimpse of a dark brown animal swimming in the water. It is a beaver.

In every ecosystem, there is a species of plant or animal that has a large effect on many other members of its community. This organism is called a **keystone**

*An ecosystem transformed: From the surrounding forest, beavers construct their sturdy dams. Once-flowing streams are turned into still ponds.*

**species**. Where they live and work, beavers are a keystone species, changing the way the Mississippi flows and the role the river plays in the ecosystem.

## Animal Architects

Beavers don't like the Mississippi. In fact, they cannot stand the sound or feel of running water. So, they use the trees in riverside forests and the river itself as tools to create the habitat they need. Beavers are North America's largest rodents, weighing up to 60 pounds (27 kg) and measuring 3 to 4 feet (.9 to 1.2 m) long. They are semiaquatic, spending part of their lives underwater and part on land as terrestrial animals. They are creatures of both aquatic and flood zone habitats. Beavers are strong swimmers, but are slow and awkward on land where they are easy prey for wolves, coyotes, bobcats, and even dogs. To protect themselves from these terrestrial predators, beavers build their homes, called lodges,

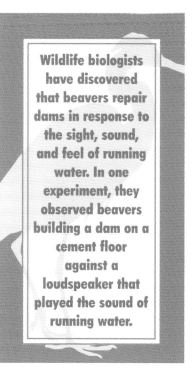

Wildlife biologists have discovered that beavers repair dams in response to the sight, sound, and feel of running water. In one experiment, they observed beavers building a dam on a cement floor against a loudspeaker that played the sound of running water.

*North America's largest rodent, the beaver is known for its thick, waterproof fur, strong teeth, and nearly nonstop chewing.*

*Safe from land-based predators, the beaver lodge has two secret, underwater entrances that lead into the center of the den. Inside the lodge, a mud platform built above the water's reach keeps the beavers dry.*

in the middle of a pond. The Mississippi isn't a pond, so the beavers must turn their stretch of the river into one. With their strong front teeth, they gnaw and fell small trees—aspen, black willow, pin cherry, and ash are among their favorites. They drag them in their mouths overland to the river or in canals they dig through the forest. At the construction site, the beavers jam the trees and tree parts into the river bottom and anchor them with rocks. Then they wedge in more sticks and stones, pack mud and grass in the cracks, and create a dam across the river.

The Mississippi River rises up behind the dam and overflows its gently sloping banks. It floods the surrounding woodland and creates a pond usually stretching between 10 and 75 acres (4–30 ha). If the pond doesn't reach the desired depth—between 3 and 4 feet (.9–1.2 m) —or if the first dam cannot hold the water back, beavers build side dams until the water level is just right for their lodge. The lodge looks like a small island piled with sticks. These sticks form the walls and ceiling of a rounded chamber about the size of a one-person tent. There is a hole in the top for air and two underwater tunnels that lead into the chamber. The mud floor of the chamber is built up from the bottom of the pond and rises above the water like an island.

Once the lodge is complete, beavers busy themselves repairing leaks and finding food to eat—mostly grass, twigs, and bark. A pair of beavers will live in a lodge, mate, and produce offspring. When the kits, or young beavers, are two years old, they leave their family to build dams and lodges of their own. Often they settle just downstream from their parents. One stretch of the river may display the construction work of several generations of beavers. Though the beaver's activities don't change the flow of the entire river, they do have a long-lasting effect on the environment in and around the ponds.

## New Neighbors

Beaver ponds destroy some parts of the river community, especially the terrestrial and flood zone plants and animals along the banks.

*Scientists are unsure why beavers will sometimes abandon trees before chewing all the way through. Most likely the trees will die, but not before playing host to a variety of fungi, wood-eating insects, and a few woodpeckers.*

Grasses and flowers drown. Animals living underground, such as mice, voles, insects, and worms, drown as well unless they can escape to higher, drier ground. Fish and insects that require flowing water may die if they become trapped in the still waters of the pond. Small trees are chewed to stumps. Trees too large for the beavers to chew or drag are left standing in the water. They die, decay, then eventually fall into the pond. Birds, owls, and squirrels nesting in these trees are forced to find new homes. And when the trees go, the shade goes, too. Sunlight pours in through new openings in the forest, and shade-seeking animals move farther away from the water.

But all is not lost. With their dams, ponds, and canals, the beavers have created two new kinds of habitat. The flowing river is now a deep pond, a different type of aquatic habitat that is a magnet for wildlife that prefer still water. As the river flows into the pond, it slows and deposits its sediment on the bottom. The pond traps organic material from upstream and from the surrounding forest. Eelgrass, lilies, duckweed, pondweed, and other aquatic plants take root or float on the surface of the pond. Ducks, geese, and other waterfowl come to the pond to eat these plants and feed on the bottom. Some are migrating waterfowl stopping at the pond to rest and feed before continuing their journey north or south. Others stay longer and may build nests around the pond to raise their young. Wood ducks take advantage of the cavities in large decaying trees to build their homes. These trees (and the many beetles and insects chewing them) also lure a variety of woodpeckers to the new beaver pond community.

Aquatic insects, such as dragonflies, water striders, mosquitoes, and whirligig beetles, thrive in the pond. As

*Safe but watchful, these wood ducklings keep an eye on their mother from the hollow of a tree.*

*Alligator snapping turtles benefit from the habitat beaver ponds provide. The water is deep enough to draw fish and ducks, some of the turtles' choice prey.*

larvae and adults, they are food for fish that prefer the deeper, cooler, oxygen-rich water. Toads, frogs, and salamanders lay their eggs in the shallow parts of pond. Muskrats, river otters, minks, frogs, and snapping turtles find homes at the edge of the pond and swim in its waters. Seasonally and in times of drought, when the upper reaches of the Mississippi may be reduced to a mere trickle, the beaver ponds remain full of water. Many animals seek this natural reservoir as a much-needed source of drinking water.

The beaver also changes the habitat around the pond. Where there once was terrestrial habitat or a habitat that was flooded every year or so, there is now a **marsh**. A marsh is a kind of wetland, a usually treeless area where the ground is saturated with water. Marshes often support a greater variety of plants and animals than in the flowing river and forest combined. This means that marshes increase the **biodiversity**, or number of different life-forms found in an ecosystem. Around the edges of the pond, grasses, rushes, cattails, and sedges take root in the marsh. These are **emergent plants** that grow with their roots and bases in wet soil or standing water for part or all of their lives.

The still waters of the marsh are ideal for many kinds of insects, especially those with aquatic larvae. Mosquitoes are probably the most famous marsh residents. Though we may consider them pests, they are an abundant source of food for birds including warblers, ducks, and red-winged blackbirds, which flock to the cattails to nest and feed. Here in the marsh, the Mississippi functions to keep the wetland wet and to deliver sediment and nutrients to the marsh's growing population.

Beaver pond reservoirs can also help minimize flooding in the areas just downstream from the dam. When the river floods upstream, the water gets distributed through the marsh where it is often absorbed by the soil there. If the deluge is extreme and the marsh becomes flooded, the water will rise up toward the top of the dam. The rising water level signals the beavers to build their dams a bit higher so the pond can hold more water. Water may run over or through the dam. Some beavers construct narrow spillways on either side of the dam to allow some of it to escape. This reduces the pressure the water places on the dam, but does not release enough water to cause flooding downstream.

*Red-winged blackbirds feed and nest in the cattails that thrive in the newly created marsh beside the pond.*

Eventually, the sediment transported by the river and deposited on the bottom begins to build up and raise the lower layers of the pond. The beavers may attempt to add to the height of the dam to deepen the pool, but in the end, the sediment wins. The pond becomes too shallow to protect the beavers in the lodge. The beavers abandon their home, and the pond and marsh slowly fill with

*In need of constant repair, dams eventually break apart and are abandoned by the beavers.*

sediment. Then a new community of plants and animals arrives. The ever-changing Mississippi resumes its original role as a flowing river.

## Damming the Mississippi

Beaver dams aren't the only barriers on the Mississippi. In fact, hundreds of man-made dams have been built along the Mississippi and its tributaries. Most of these dams were built in the 1920s and 1930s by the United States Army Corps of Engineers to raise the level of the river between Minneapolis, Minnesota, and St. Louis, Missouri, to create a navigation channel deep enough for heavy barge traffic. The Corps of Engineers constructed 29 dams over 670 miles (1,072 km) of river to raise the water level from an average of 3 feet (.9 m) to 9 feet (2.7 m). The dams were also built to create reservoirs that would hold a permanent supply of water for towns and farms even when the river was low. They were also designed to prevent flooding as excess water from upstream could be stored in the reservoir, then slowly released downstream through spillways on the sides of the dam.

When these dams were constructed, floods drowned thousands of acres of the floodplain habitat. And, like the beaver dams, they created new habitats—deep pools, marshes, side channels, and other backwaters. But sediments from upland areas have been filling in these productive habitats. Sediment and nutrients that would normally flow downstream are now being trapped behind the dams. Here they settle, gradually building up the river bottom. But humans don't abandon their dams. Instead, they use a tool the beaver never dreamed of: dredges. These huge machines scoop out the sediment and other material on the river bottom to increase the depth of the water. Much of this dredged sediment was deposited in the shallow aquatic and flood zone habitats in the floodplain. In many places these areas became terrestrial habitats and lost their ability to absorb floodwaters and reduce downstream flooding.

*Dams and navigation locks—a total of twenty-nine on the main channel of the Mississippi—deepen the river for the passage of large boats and store water for surrounding cities and towns.*

33

# The Great Floods

Oceans of brown riverwater surge through the middle of a small town. Water flows in through the doors and windows of homes, schools, and businesses. Cars are stranded, abandoned, and half-submerged in water. The water rises up the poles of street signs and stoplights. It creeps up the walls of sandbags people have piled around their homes. The town is being evacuated. The streets are now rivers for small motorboats rescuing homeowners and some of their belongings. Tearful families leave their ruined homes behind. Farmers gaze out over their fields, now covered in brown lakes that have drowned their newly sprouted crops of corn, wheat, and soybeans. The Mississippi is flooding.

For most of us, the word *flood* means a disaster. It suggests human suffering, the loss of property, and in some cases, the loss of life. It indicates the river is out of control. These extreme floods, which are often destructive, occur only every one hundred to five hundred years on the Mississippi. More typical floods occur every year, usually in the spring. These regular seasonal floods create flood zone habitats where the river and the land meet. Here, the river alternates between low and high water, and the land accommodates

*Flooding is a natural phenomenon, but the Great Flood of 1993 on the upper Mississippi was one of the worst in history. Human lives, property, and confidence in flood-control measures were all lost.*

both wet and dry seasons. Many plants and animals live here and depend on the changing fortunes of life in the flood zone.

## The Floodplain Forest

North of St. Louis, Missouri, you can visit a forest growing in the flood zone of the Mark Twain National Wildlife Refuge. This is not an ordinary forest. It is composed of **flood-tolerant** trees—those that can survive being covered by water for long periods. Not only do they tolerate it—they benefit from it. The trees closest to the river are the black willows. They are shrublike trees growing in narrow bands along the banks. During the spring floods, their trunks and lower branches are often submerged. Their roots are surrounded by soil that is saturated with water. This would kill most trees as the water cuts off the necessary oxygen supply to the roots. The trees normally drown. But the willows are different. Their roots are fibrous (fiberlike) and thus have more air spaces that can hold more oxygen. Willow roots also grow near the surface. This helps stabilize them in saturated soil and puts them closer to the dry soil after the floodwater recedes.

Willow branches break easily in the strong currents of the floodwater. But the willows make the most of this loss: the snapped-off limbs root easily in the soft soil of the riverbank. The flood often brings with it heavy loads of sediment that bury these broken branches. When the waters recede in summer, the riverbanks will then sprout with new willows. When the willow trunk is buried in sediment, the trunk itself sprouts roots near the surface of the soil. The willow roots, trunks, and lower branches help trap and stabilize the mucky sediments left behind after a flood. Over time, the soil may build up beneath the willows. The band of willows then has room to expand, marching forward, closer and closer toward the river. The silver maples are following close behind.

Silver maples are one of the most abundant trees along the Mississippi River. They have the same flood-tolerant adaptations as the willow, but they cannot be submerged by floodwater for as long a period of time. So they grow on the slightly drier soil behind the willows. The flooding benefits the silver maples in several ways. It scours the floodplain, often wiping out the grasses and other competing

*Receding floodwaters leave behind soft, saturated soil—the ideal conditions for silver maple seeds to sprout.*

vegetation. It deposits new sediments that are rich in nutrients. It leaves behind soil that is moist and soft—the perfect place for a seed. Silver maples produce an enormous quantity of winged seeds that often blanket the soil after the floodwater recedes. Most trees' seeds require a cold period before they can begin sprouting; they drop off the tree in the fall, lie dormant on the ground through the winter, then sprout in the spring. But not the silver maples. Their seeds can sprout in late spring or summer as soon as the floodwaters recede. The seedlings grow quickly and will eventually shade out the willows that built up the new soil in which the silver maples sprout.

## A Flood without Forests

These trees benefit from flooding, and during a flood people benefit from the trees. Runoff from spring rainfall or snowmelt often flows

*Sunlight glistens on the lingering floodwaters of 1993. Depending on their species and size, floodplain trees may survive being submerged for up to three years.*

across saturated land as it makes its way toward the Mississippi and its tributaries. When this runoff enters the forest, the roots, fallen branches, and layers of decaying leaves break this flow of water, slow it down, and trap it in the forest. The water then seeps into the ground where it is absorbed by the soil and soaked up by the trees. Runoff that passes through floodplain forests often never makes it to the Mississippi River.

Root systems help hold the soil together so that runoff and river currents do not erode the banks. But not all floodplains have forests. Beginning in the nineteenth century, much of the floodplain forest was harvested for firewood and for lumber used for homes and buildings. Once the trees were cleared, towns and cities were built. Farmers discovered the rich soils of the floodplain, and soon crops replaced trees. Without the forests, what was going to stop the flooding? Levees.

Reinforced earthen walls called **levees** were built parallel to the river to keep the water from reaching the floodplain farms and towns. As more and more levees were built, the river's sediment load could not be spread thinly across the floodplain. Instead, it became trapped between the levees and raised the level of the river. For the most part, the levees worked—until the Great Flood of 1993.

It began in the fall of 1992 when heavy rains fell across many of the midwestern states that drain into the upper Mississippi River. The ground was already wet when winter arrived with heavy snow and rain. The soil was saturated. The rains of the following spring and summer couldn't soak into the ground. They flowed directly into tributary streams and rivers, which began to swell and flood. Severe thunderstorms and record-breaking rainfalls hit the region for weeks. The Mississippi rose up the sides of thousands of levees, flowed over them, and once again found its way to the floodplain. Here, it engulfed entire towns and farms, destroying 70,500 homes and damaging 149,000 others. It swallowed highways, bridges, and railroad tracks. It took 52 human lives and left 74,000 people homeless. In November, the river finally returned to normal levels. By then the flood had caused more than $15 billion worth of damage to 20 million acres (8.1 million ha) of land, including the floodplain forests.

*Sandbags were used to build temporary walls to keep the floodwaters at bay. When emergency strikes a riverside community, everyone pitches in.*

Floodplain forests can tolerate brief floods, but the Great Flood of 1993 took the lives of many trees. The less flood-tolerant trees, such as hackberry and sugarberry, died after standing in water for several months. Many trees did not grow leaves in the spring after the flood. Even the most flood-tolerant trees were pushed to their limits, especially the smaller ones. Many young trees were simply uprooted and washed away. Despite these losses, much of the forest was recovering by the next spring, especially the hearty black willows and silver maples.

## Restoring Spunky Bottoms

The Great Flood of 1993 has changed the way many people look at the relationship between the river and its floods. People began to ask questions: Would the flood have been less destructive if the river had been allowed to overflow its banks naturally? Should levees be removed? Although the Flood of 1993 was classified as a five-hundred-year event, should people continue to live, work, and farm on the floodplain? Some people decided no. They rebuilt their homes and relocated their towns out of reach of the river. Farmers abandoned their flooded fields and planted on higher ground where future floods couldn't reach them.

These questions and responses concerned not only the Mississippi River, but also many of its tributaries that flooded in 1993. On the Illinois River, at a place called Spunky Bottoms, there was a 1,157-acre (462-ha) farm where corn and soybeans once grew. Though it was protected by levees, groundwater surfaced in the fields, and the levees weren't always effective. Efforts to control the water levels with pumps and ditches were expensive and ultimately ineffective. So, after several soggy years and a poor farm economy, the farm was sold in 1997 to a national conservation group. Their goal is to restore Spunky Bottom's native plant and wildlife communities and to reconnect the river to its floodplain.

What's in store for Spunky Bottoms is a mosaic of habitats including open water, marshes, floodplain forests, and prairies. The first phase of the work began at the end of 1998, when huge pumps that drained water from the fields were turned off. This allowed the water naturally seeping up from the ground and from tributary streams to fill in the fields. Eventually the water level will rise to match the level of the river on the other side of the levee. As this happens, the water and the land will merge into a variety of wetland environments.

Many plant communities will reestablish themselves from seeds dormant in the soil, blown in from nearby fields or carried from upstream tributaries. But some planting is necessary. In the spring of

1999, more than 600 pounds (270 kg) of seeds were planted in one section of prairie. These included flowering plants such as clover, sunflower, coneflower, and goldenrod and wild grasses such as rye, bluestem, and switchgrass. These are just a few of the 236 different plants that will be reintroduced at Spunky Bottoms.

Once the water level on the property is approximately equal to that in the river, a controllable gateway will be installed in the levee to directly link the river to its floodplain. Through this levee, the water will replenish the marshes, backwater lakes, and pools. Aquatic organisms will enter the floodplain, too. Fish, amphibians, and reptiles will use these wetlands for reproduction, feeding, raising their young, and overwintering. When the Mississippi on the other side of the levee floods, the gate will be opened to let Spunky Bottoms flood, too.

The many scientists working on the project are carefully watching the land as it changes in response to increased water levels, rainfall, runoff, and its new plant

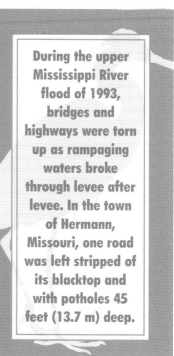

During the upper Mississippi River flood of 1993, bridges and highways were torn up as rampaging waters broke through levee after levee. In the town of Hermann, Missouri, one road was left stripped of its blacktop and with potholes 45 feet (13.7 m) deep.

*Nighttime prowlers and scavengers, raccoons are one sign of an ecosystem's renewed health.*

*Workers plant saplings as part of the restoration of Spunky Bottoms, a floodplain forest in the making.*

communities. They are watching the return of insects, birds, and small mammals. While scientists can make predictions about what will happen at Spunky Bottoms, there is no way of knowing for certain until it actually happens. It is a thousand-acre experiment conducted by a team of knowledgeable scientists. If successful, Spunky Bottoms will become an ecosystem—and an example for future projects aimed at restoring the lost floodplains of the river.

# Booming Backwaters

The early spring rains have finally let up. The sun is shining in Tennessee, and you plan to spend the day with your family on the Mississippi River. You tie the canoe on top of the car, pack your paddles, your fishing poles, and some sandwiches and lemonade for lunch. The car is loaded and you're ready to go. One last thing: you quickly write a note and tape it to your front door—Gone Fishing. Just when it seems like you're never going to get there, you see the entrance to Chickasaw National Wildlife Refuge. This 22,378-acre (8,951 ha) refuge lies on the Mississippi's floodplain. As you approach the refuge, the car stops. Everyone gets out to look at the road ahead. It is completely covered in water. Flooded. And so is all the land ahead of you. The heavy rainfall has brought the river over its banks and up onto the land. You eat your picnic lunch in the car on the way home.

The following weekend, you return to the refuge. The landscape is completely different. The floodwater has receded, but it hasn't taken all its water with it. It has left behind numerous lakes, small pools, and lots of puddles. These still waters are full of life: fish, frogs,

*The Mississippi draws outdoor lovers from all around. Here, nothing disturbs the water but the paddle of a lone canoeist.*

toads, salamanders, and countless other aquatic creatures. Many of these creatures benefit from time spent in a still-water habitat. Others depend on such habitats for survival. But you can't see any of them from your car.

## Calling All Amphibians!

As you hike through the soggy floodplain forest toward the river, you encounter dozens of shallow pools nearly hidden among the towering cypress, tupelo, sweet gum, and pecan trees. You jump over a few,

*Floodwaters often leave behind shallow pools that become critical breeding and nursery habitats for a variety of woodland amphibians.*

*Like other amphibians, tiger salamanders absorb water through their skin and require a moist habitat. They feed on insects, worms, snails and other small animals, including members of their own species.*

then stop at one for a closer look. You are as still and quiet as the pool. You watch frogs swimming beneath the surface, pairs of half-submerged toads, and strings and clumps of small, jellylike eggs. Tadpoles congregate at the edge of the pool. You think you see a salamander partially hidden in the decaying leaves in the bottom. How did they all get here? Can they all live in this pond together?

This water hole is an **ephemeral pool**, or temporary pool. It has other names, too: spring pool, vernal pool, and disappearing pond. It will hold water for a few months in the early spring and summer. By late summer, it dries up as the water in it evaporates or is taken up by trees as they leaf out. It is their temporary nature that makes them an unusual habitat for animals. Frogs, toads, salamanders, and tadpole shrimp use these pools in the spring and early summer then return to the forest or into the sediment at the bottom of the pond until the next flood. These creatures are part of a **pulsed ecosystem**, that is, one that alternates between wet and dry periods. For amphibians these pools are important breeding habitat because their eggs and larvae require water. The drying of the pool in summer makes it an unsuitable habitat for fish. But fish are the main predators in the pools that are close to the river and thus easier to access.

*This leopard frog is in its final stage of development. Soon its tail will be completely absorbed.*

Many frogs hop out of their winter woodland homes to find mates in and around the ephemeral pools. After a few weeks of often raucous mating calls, the males usually find a female. Once they mate the female lays hundreds of eggs in a mass, often in a huge communal cluster with other frogs' egg masses. These are easy to spot in the water. From these eggs, tadpoles hatch and begin their spring marathon: they must grow and develop into adult frogs by the time the pool dries up. When there is no more water left in the pool (or before that if they are ready), the young frogs crawl out and hop toward the moist woodland.

The pool is also a valued habitat for a variety of salamanders. They spend most of their secretive lives in the forest in underground tunnels or burrows dug by small mammals. The can also burrow under rocks, logs, and forest debris. Every year, they migrate to the ephemeral pools to mate, lay their clusters of eggs, and then return to the forest. In some cases, the eggs are laid near the surface of the water where algae begins to grow on them. The algae supply oxygen to the developing salamanders. This raises the salamanders' chances ofsurvival. This could be critical in a pool with a limited amount of dissolved oxygen. Within several weeks, young salamanders emerge from the eggs. They closely resemble adults, but they have gills for obtaining oxygen from the water. Young salamanders spend much of their youth in the pool, feeding on aquatic insects, tadpoles, and in some cases each other.

By midsummer, the amphibians have grown up and left the pool.

*Tadpole shrimp spend their entire lives in the pool. Eggs that spend the winter on the dry bottom will hatch the following spring.*

But the pool is not empty. It might be full of tadpole shrimp. These crustaceans measure about an inch long (1.6 cm) and resemble miniature horseshoe crabs you might see along the Atlantic coast. These shrimp mature, mate, lay eggs, and die all in one season in the pool. Sometimes the eggs hatch the same year they are laid. Often, the eggs sink to the bottom of the pool where they remain in the sediment throughout the winter. They will hatch the next spring when the water returns.

By late summer, our pool has disappeared. It has served its purpose: providing a place for a small community of amphibians and tadpole shrimp to mate and breed. When dry in the summer and fall, it is an easily overlooked feature of the forest. It is a mere depression on the forest floor, but a collection basin for dying plants and autumn leaves that will begin to decay and provide nutrients for next year's residents when the floods come again.

## Lakes Alive

Now it is time to start paddling. You and your family haul the canoe down to a lake and begin a relaxing afternoon exploring this still stretch of the Mississippi River. The lake you are on is called an **oxbow lake**. You can find these oxbows easily on a map. They are the C-shaped bodies of water next to the river. These lakes used to be part of the main channel along a twisty, winding leg of the river. But as the water slowed going around the bends, or meanders, it deposited sediment at each end of the curve. As large amounts of sediment gradually built up, the current slowed even more. A river always seeks the shortest, fastest route to its mouth. Eventually, the river deposits so much silt at the ends of the meander that it shores up a pocket of water, cut off from the main channel. The river then carves out a new straight channel that bypasses the curve and actually shortens the length of the river. The abandoned meander then becomes an oxbow lake.

As long as the main channel remains close to the oxbow, the river can flow into it during floods. This serves to scour out the sediments in the lake and to replenish it with a new supply of water. However, as the river continues to shift its course away from the lake, only extreme floods reach the lake, if at all. During its life so close to

*The Mississippi is constantly changing its path as it winds toward the delta. Its former course can be traced in abandoned meanders and C-shaped oxbow lakes.*

the river, the oxbow lake is one of the most productive habitats in the river ecosystem.

At Chickasaw National Wildlife Refuge, the Mississippi has not completely forgotten its oxbows. There are no levees here, and the lake receives floodwaters annually. The floodwaters also bring aquatic

*Bluegills rarely grow more than 10 inches (25 cm). Females clear out a nest on the bottom of the pool and guard the eggs against predators.*

plants, fish, macroinvertebrates, and other aquatic creatures along for the ride, as well as a heavy load of sediment and nutrients from upstream. When the river returns to its channel, it takes some of the old lakewater with it. Then the sediment settles to the bottom, and the lake becomes an ideal food factory. Sunlight and nutrients in the water nourish algae, which grow on the surface of the lake and as far down as the light reaches. The algae become food for microscopic animals called **zooplankton.**

Larger life-forms settle in the lake, too. Benthic (bottom-dwelling) creatures such as macroinvertebrates may burrow into the sediments, find a rock to crawl under, or swim freely in the water. These organisms are food for a variety of fish, including gizzard shad,

bluegill, bass, crappie, and catfish that arrive during spawning (egg-laying) season with the floodwaters. As river dwellers, these fish usually seek the slower waters or pools within the river for spawning. But here in the lake, it's all prime spawning territory. In the calm waters, they mate and lay their eggs, which become food for many aquatic creatures. In about three days, the surviving eggs hatch and the fry, or young fish, feed on zooplankton. When they grow larger, they feed on insects and may eat other fish in the lake.

In a very short time, the fish population has boomed. When the river floods again the following spring, it will take many of these fish with it. The Mississippi replenishes the lake with new water, and the oxbow replenishes the Mississippi with an abundance of young fish, ready to handle life in a free-flowing river.

The Mississippi River supports a wealth of fish representing over 260 freshwater species. By comparison, a lake in the midwestern United States might support fewer than fifteen species. This great abundance and variety of fish in the Mississippi is due in part to the wide range of habitats the river provides. One of the most critical and productive habitats is on the floodplain, where lakes and backwaters offer calm and protected waters for spawning adults and young fish alike.

## Going, Going, Gone

Oxbow lakes and ephemeral pools are rapidly disappearing from the Mississippi floodplain. The oxbows eventually die as they fill up with sediment and cease to be lakes altogether. This is a natural process, but the increased amount of sediment carried by the river is speeding it up. The sediment load gets heavier and heavier as the river moves downstream. By the time the Mississippi reaches Tennessee, it is carrying sediment from seven states. When the oxbows disappear, they will not be replaced with new ones. The levees along most of the Mississippi prevent the river from abandoning its current meandering channel to take any new shortcuts to the sea.

Ephemeral pools are disappearing from the landscape, too. As wetlands along the Mississippi are developed for agriculture or real estate, the vernal pools are bulldozed over or drained along with the rest of the wetlands. As ephemeral pools disappear permanently, so

*As their name implies, channel catfish can be found in the Mississippi's main channel. But they also thrive in oxbow lakes. Their "whiskers" are an adaptation that helps them find their way in the murky water.*

will the community of creatures that depends on them. These pools occur along the Mississippi and in many wetlands across the country. Because most people consider ephemeral pools just "big puddles" of no particular value, scientists are working to educate the public about these fragile and fleeting habitats before it is too late.

# Watching the Water

You can learn a lot about your local stream by taking a walk around your neighborhood or schoolyard and using just a few tools and your powers of observation. You should wear rain boots or old shoes and travel with a friend or a supervising adult.

Materials:
- notebook
- pencil or pen

1. During a rainfall, try to follow the path of the rain as it flows off the roofs of the houses and buildings in your neighborhood. Watch your streets, sidewalks, paved playgrounds, and parking lots to follow the flow of the water. Does it flow into storm drains below the road or sidewalk? Does it run onto the land and soak into the soil? Where do the drains lead? As you walk toward the stream, you will most likely be following the same path the water makes from your home or school. Draw a simple map tracing the path of the water.

2. At the stream, look around. What kind of trees or plants do you see on the banks? Are there signs of human impact nearby such as agriculture, housing, industry, roadways, or building construction?

3. Does the water have a strange odor? A chemical smell can mean harmful pollutants have entered the stream. A rotten egg smell can mean sewage is getting into the stream.

4. Looking at the stream, does the water appear clear or cloudy? If it is cloudy, it may be carrying a heavy load of sediment from upstream.

5. Is the surface of the water covered in green slime? This is algae, which can deplete the oxygen in the stream. Is the surface of the water shiny or rainbow colored? This is most likely oil, which may be from roadways, sewers, or an oil pipeline leak.

6. What does the stream bottom look like? Is it solid rock, loose rocks of various sizes, sandy, or muddy? If it is rocky, are the rocks covered with sediment? In a healthy stream, the rocks should look like they were placed on the surface of the streambed, not buried in it.

7. If your stream has no strange odors and is free from abundant algae and surface oil, proceed to turn over a few rocks in the stream. Are there any insects on the underside of the rocks? This is one sign of a healthy stream. Do you see fish or other small aquatic creatures in the water? Are there animal tracks along the banks of the river or signs of birds nearby? Why might these animals live near the stream?

8. Is there trash in the stream? What might be the source of this trash?

9. Does the stream have a smell? How does the smell compare with your drinking water?

10. Write down your observations. Try to visit your stream during different seasons and make note of changes such as the amount of sediment or trash in the stream. Look at the land around the stream, has it changed in ways that help or hurt the stream?

# The Dynamic Delta

*Y*ou are driving southeast from the city of New Orleans along the highway that follows the Mississippi to the Gulf of Mexico. On either side of you, two massive levees line the river. This is land that the Mississippi River began building six hundred years ago from clay, silt, sand, and gravel it has lifted from thirty-one states and two Canadian provinces. For six hundred years the river has deposited sediment here at its mouth as it slowed upon entering the Gulf of Mexico. This is the Mississippi's **delta**, the flat, low-lying plain at the mouth of the river. You stop the car at a town called Venice. The river continues, but the road does not. The salty smell of the ocean leads you on. You get in a boat and head toward Delta National Wildlife Refuge where the Mississippi meets the sea.

## Sanctuary by the Sea

The refuge resembles a giant jigsaw puzzle of marshes, mudflats, sluggish creeks, and open water. The river doesn't surge through the refuge as much as it flows gently in and out with the ocean's tides. As the ocean edges in at high tide, it brings salt water into the delta. At low tide, the ocean draws the freshwater out of the

*As the Mississippi nears the end of its journey in Louisiana, it flows in many channels and rivulets through the marshlands of the delta.*

river channels. The area of the delta where the salt and fresh water mix is called an **estuary**. Because the water here is gentle, shallow, and sunlit, many fish and shellfish use it as a nursery, or a place to spend the early stages of their life. They might pass their adult life in the open waters of the gulf, but they move here into the protected waters of the delta to increase their chances of survival.

Adult shrimp live in the open ocean of the Gulf of Mexico, where they mate and lay eggs. The female shrimp may lay from 1,500 to 14,000 eggs several miles offshore. The eggs and tiny hatched larvae are then washed into the marsh by the ocean tide. Here, the larvae spend the first few months of their lives, feeding on the detritus-rich waters of the saltwater marsh. Because the water here is shallow and brackish (partly salty and partly fresh), the shrimp are safe from many of the larger saltwater fish that prey on them. When they have grown to be a few inches long, they swim back to the gulf where they will spend the rest of their lives.

In addition to shrimp, the saltwater marshes and waterways support oysters, blue crabs, and a diversity of fish, including speckled trout, redfish, and flounder. The freshwater areas of the refuge support

*The warm, brackish waters of the marshlands support a bounty of crawfish, a favorite food of wading birds and a major resource for the seafood industry.*

catfish, largemouth bass, and many kinds of sunfish. The predominant plants in the freshwater areas are elephant ear, wild millet, delta three-square, roseau cane, and delta duck potato.

You can't find a plant with a name like "delta duck potato" and not have any ducks around. In fact, the refuge attracts hundreds of thousands of ducks representing eighteen different species. Mallards, green-winged teal, gadwalls, and northern pintails congregate here for the winter. They have flown great distances from colder climates of the northern United States and Canada. During the winter the ducks and geese feed on many of the aquatic plants (including the duck potato), snails, small insects, and crustaceans living in the marsh. Biologists and birders have recorded more than 400,000 ducks and geese at the refuge during the wintertime.

In the spring, they return to the north via a route that is well known to them—the Mississippi flyway. This great migratory route, the most traveled of the four major bird migration routes in North America, is shaped like an enormous funnel with its tip at the Louisiana coast. The neck of the funnel leads up the Mississippi River, then begins to widen on either side until it spans practically the entire continent at its mouth—from Alaska to the eastern shores of Canada's Hudson Bay. With its north-south orientation, the flyway functions as a pathway between breeding and wintering areas for nearly three hundred bird species, including ducks, geese, swans, pelicans, cormorants, and untold numbers of songbirds and shorebirds. Along their migration route, these birds use the Mississippi River, its tributaries, and its floodplain habitats for food and rest stops.

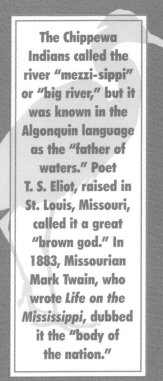

The Chippewa Indians called the river "mezzi-sippi" or "big river," but it was known in the Algonquin language as the "father of waters." Poet T. S. Eliot, raised in St. Louis, Missouri, called it a great "brown god." In 1883, Missourian Mark Twain, who wrote *Life on the Mississippi*, dubbed it the "body of the nation."

## More Sediment, Please

The delta relies on the sediment the Mississippi River carries from the North. These particles, which formed the delta hundreds of years ago, are needed to continue building up the marshes and mudflats

*Great egrets often nest together in large colonies. The female usually lays three to five light blue or light green eggs. When the babies hatch, they are covered with down and tended by both parents.*

that exist here today. The Mississippi carries an estimated 300 to 400 billion tons (272–363 metric tons) of sediment past New Orleans, Louisiana, each year. This is about half the amount carried in the 1950s. Artificial and natural levees lining the banks of the river have prevented the sediment and freshwater from spilling over into the

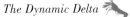

delta. Dredging has deepened the channels and increased the speed of the river's current. Without time to settle onto the bottom, much of the sediment flows past the delta and is deposited directly into the deep waters of the gulf. As a result, from 1956 to 1978, approximately 51 percent of the freshwater marshes in the Mississippi's active delta disappeared, converted to open water.

In 1978, the Mississippi River flooded at the refuge and caused several breaks in the natural levees there. Floodwater poured through the openings and deposited its sediment in open-water ponds. The sediment built up quickly into fan-shaped slopes called splays. In some splays, the elevation of the delta increased 6 inches (12 cm) a year. Emergent plants then sprang up on the splays, and in just a few years wintering waterfowl began using the splays for feeding and resting areas.

Since this natural success story happened, wildlife managers at the refuge have created thirty-four additional splays by cutting through the natural levees that guide the river to the sea. In the past five years, these and other efforts at the refuge have created over 2,200 additional acres (880 ha) of land in open-water areas for waterbirds to use.

As the wildlife managers at the refuge are allowing more sediment into the marshes they are struggling against the oil and gas companies. With the discovery in the 1930s of these natural resources in the waters of the gulf, oil and gas companies quickly moved in. More than half of the refuge's 48,800 acres (19,520 ha) is leased by oil and gas companies, which dig canals that give access to drilling sites for oil tankers and other large vessels. The sediments dug from the canals were piled high on the banks of the river. This smothered and destroyed much of the vegetation that held the banks firmly in place. The increase in boat traffic through the canals also produces waves that crash against the banks of the canals. With fewer plants along the edges, the waves sweep in and erode the soft sediments that form the banks. These straight, wide, deepened canals slice through the marshes and also create another problem. Salt water is able to penetrate far deeper into the marsh than it normally would through the mazelike natural waterways of the refuge.

 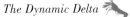

*Since oil and gas were discovered in the Gulf of Mexico in the 1930s, refineries and large-scale machinery have become part of the delta landscape.*

As the salt water mixes with the freshwater areas of the refuge, the balance of the estuary changes dramatically. Plants that are not salt-tolerant quickly die. Freshwater fish and other aquatic animals die as well or crowd into ever-shrinking habitats. The increase in saltwater habitat has caused a boom in populations of saltwater species, such as shrimp, crab, and lobsters. This is good news for the delta fishermen who rely on saltwater fish and shellfish for their livelihood. But scientists worry that a boom in Louisiana's seafood industry may end up as a bust in the long run. The U.S. Fish and Wildlife Service, which manages many of the coastal wildlife refuges, reports that total seafood production in the wetlands remains strong, but only because there are a record number of boats in the water.

Yields per individual boat have fallen an estimated 90 percent since the 1940s.

The invasion of salt water has increased in recent years as the delta has been slowly sinking and shrinking. With less and less new sediment from the Mississippi River, the ocean is free to move farther and farther inland. Scientists report that for the past thirty years, the Louisiana marshes have rated as the continent's fastest-shrinking landmass. One area of coastal marshes and wetlands created by the delta 3,900 years ago is disappearing at the rate of eight square miles (20 sq. km) a year. The restoration efforts at Delta National Wildlife Refuge have been effective in creating new marshlands, but this may be too weak an effort against the encroaching sea and a river that is not allowed to rebuild its deltas.

*The balance of salt and freshwater in the delta is key to the survival of shrimp, as well as those whose livelihood depends on a strong harvest.*

# Tomorrow's Mississippi

The Mississippi River ecosystem has been changing for tens of thousands of years. Using water and sediment as its tools, the river is constantly creating and then destroying what it builds. It changes its channel, floods its banks, erodes land, forms islands, constructs deltas, and replenishes marshes. These changes are considered part of the natural life of a river. The communities of plants and animals adjust and adapt to these changes. They, too, are part of the river.

Today, changes are occurring much more quickly. In the last 150 years, people have altered the river enormously. We have contaminated its water, cleared its forests, taken over its floodplain, reshaped its channel, dammed it, dumped sediment into it, and dredged sediment out of it. We have used its resources without thinking about renewing them.

Whose problems are these? Even though the Mississippi flows through our nation's heartland, it is largely a forgotten river. It is so large that no state, no government, or no single organization claims responsibility for it. The Mississippi is tied to every person living and working in the 1,234,700 square miles (3,197,873 sq. km) of land drained by the river and its tributaries. Problems that occur throughout this vast area end up making their way to the river. A polluted

*The future of the Mississippi is cloudy: Can we balance growing human dependency on the river with the needs of its organisms?*

stream in Pennsylvania, too much fertilizer in Iowa, hazardous waste illegally dumped from a factory in St. Louis, urban growth in Wisconsin, and deforestation in Minnesota all mean trouble for the Mississippi River.

Clearly, taking care of the Mississippi is a big job. Fortunately, in the last twenty-five years people have become more concerned with the health of the Mississippi ecosystem. They have also become more willing to do something about it. Since 1972 and the passage of the Clean Water Act, state and local governments and agencies have been working together with hundreds of private organizations to meet higher standards for the Mississippi River and its tributaries. Wetland restoration projects progress in various stretches of the river. Volunteer groups organizing river and stream clean-ups are active in all of the thirty-one states that drain to the Mississippi. Progress is slow, but it will take time to

*Recreation and transportation: Human activity impacts the Mississippi's ecosystem in countless ways.*

undo much of the damage of the last 150 years. And it takes time to learn how to treat a river so it can function as a healthy ecosystem.

No matter how hard people work, the Mississippi will never look as it did when European explorers first laid eyes on it. Humans have changed the river in permanent ways. The dams, the levees, the riverfront cities and towns, and the barges are here to stay. They, too, are a part of the Mississippi River ecosystem. The future of the Mississippi depends on our ability to balance our needs with the needs of the other living things in the ecosystem. We need corn and soybeans, but do we need to plant it next to the river? We need oil and natural gas, but do we need more channels through the marshes of the delta? Our factories need great quantities of coal and petroleum, but do they need to be transported on the river? And how much drinking water can we expect the Mississippi to supply? The answers to these and many more questions will help us make wise decisions about how we treat the mighty Mississippi to be certain its future is mighty as well.

*Barges the size of football fields ply the Mississippi, shipping supplies and materials to riverfront cities such as New Orleans, Louisiana.*

# Glossary

**adaptation**  the special features that help organisms survive in a particular environment.

**aquatic**  relating to or living in water.

**benthic macroinvertebrate**  a group of spineless aquatic animals that dwell on the bottom of streams, rivers, and other bodies of water.

**biodiversity**  the variety of plant and animal species in an area. Beavers increase the biodiversity of the areas where they build their dams as they create marshes.

**biological community**  all of the organisms that live together and interact in a particular environment.

**channel**  the part of a river that is deepest and carries the most water.

**delta**  the flat, low-lying plain at the mouth of a river.

**detritus**  freshly dead or partially decomposed remains of plants and animals.

**detrivore**  an animal that feeds on detritus.

**ecology**  the study of the relationships among species and their environment. A person who studies ecology is called an ecologist.

**ecosystem**  the association of living things in a biological community, plus their interactions with the nonliving parts of the environment.

**emergent plants**  organisms that grow with their roots and bases in wet soil or water for part or all of their lives. Marsh plants, such as rushes and cattails, are emergent plants.

**estuary**  the area, usually a bay, where salt water from the ocean mixes with freshwater from a river.

**floodplain**  the usually flat land next to a river that is subject to flooding.

**flood tolerant**  the ability of a plant to survive being covered in water for long periods.

**flood zone habitat**  the area of a river's floodplain that is regularly flooded and creates a habitat that is alternately wet, soggy, or dry for all or parts of the year.

**food chain**  a pathway that describes feeding relationships in which one organism is eaten by another organism that is, in turn, eaten by another.

**habitat**  the place that has all the living and nonliving things that an organism needs to live and grow.

**keystone species**  a species that has a large effect on many species in its community or ecosystem.

**levee**  a bank which keeps a river from overflowing its channel. The Mississippi River builds its own levees, but most levees are man-made reinforced earthen walls.

**marsh**  a usually treeless area where the ground is saturated with water. A marsh is a type of wetland.

**organism**  a living thing, such as a plant, animal, or fungus.

**photosynthesis**  the process by which plants and some other organisms that have chlorophyll use sunlight, carbon dioxide, and water to make sugars and other substances.

**phytoplankton**  tiny floating plants. Also known as algae, they create their own energy from the sun and provide food for many other organisms in the food chain.

**predator**  an animal that kills other animals for food.

**runoff**  rainwater, snowmelt, and other water that runs off the surface of the land instead of soaking into the soil.

**sediment**  fine particles of sand, silt, and clay.

**tributary**  a stream or river that flows into a larger stream or river.

# Further Exploration

Badt, Karin Luisa. *The Mississippi Flood of 1993*. Chicago: Childrens Press, n.d.

Challand, Helen. *Disappearing Wetlands*. Chicago: Childrens Press, 1992

Grall, George. "The Pools of Spring." *National Geographic*, April 1999

Holling, Clancy. *Minn of the Mississippi*. Boston: Houghton-Mifflin, 1951.

Mitchell, John. "Our Polluted Runoff." *National Geographic*, February 1996.

Pielou, E. C. *Fresh Water*. Chicago: University of Chicago Press, 1998.

Pollard, Michael. *The Mississippi*. Tarrytown, NY: Benchmark Books, 1997

Sayre, April Pulley. *River and Stream*. New York: Henry Holt & Co., 1996

Sayre, April Pulley. *Wetland*. New York: Henry Holt & Co., 1996

Twain, Mark. *Life on the Mississippi*. New York: Penguin Books, 1984

## On the Internet

www.americanrivers.com
www.epa.gov.owow
www.riverwatch.org

## Organizations

Chickasaw National
Wildlife Refuge
1505 Sand Bluff Rd.
Ripley, TN 38063
(901) 635-7621

Delta National Wildlife
Refuge
Southeast Louisiana
Refuges
1010 Gause Blvd.
Slidell, LA 70458
(504) 534-2235

Lake Itasca State Park
HC 05 Box 4
Lake Itasca, MN 56470
(218) 266-2100

Mark Twain National
Wildlife Refuge
1704 N. 24th St.
Quincy, IL 62301
(217) 224-8580

The Nature Conservancy
Illinois Chapter
Great Rivers Area Office
220 W. Main St.
Havanna, IL 62644
(309) 543-6502

# Index

Page numbers for illustrations are in **boldface**.